Children Sermons

*Booster
Shots for a
Healthy Soul*

B. Lynn Chesnutt

WESTBOW
PRESS®
A DIVISION OF THOMAS NELSON
& ZONDERVAN

WestBow Press books may be ordered through booksellers or by contacting:

WestBow Press
A Division of Thomas Nelson & Zondervan
1663 Liberty Drive
Bloomington, IN 47403
www.westbowpress.com
1 (866) 928-1240

ISBN: 978-1-5127-5753-8 (sc)
ISBN: 978-1-5127-5755-2 (hc)
ISBN: 978-1-5127-5754-5 (e)

Library of Congress Control Number: 2016916200

Print information available on the last page.

WestBow Press rev. date: 10/7/2016

CONTENTS

To My Grandchildren:

Zachary DeWhite

Noah Jeffrey

Nicole Marie

Justin Emanuel

Taylor Wimberley

Malyssa Lynn

Virgil Howard

Joel Vincent

David Alphonso

Let the little children come to me, and do
not hinder them, for the kingdom of God
belongs to such as these.

—Luke 18:16

ACKNOWLEDGMENTS

God, whose Word lives perpetually with us; and whose love grants mercy and grace for all our endeavors.

Church family members: Wanda Williamson for editing, taking the photograph of my hands for the sermon prayers, and encouragement, and Oceola Brisco for the photograph of the bouquet with lily used for the "Onions and Lilies" scripture page.

My granddaughter Malyssa Lynn Lipscomb for allowing me to use one of her first drawings, "A Brother with His Sisters," for the inside cover.

My son Joel V. Smoot, Sr. for writing "The Shoe Shine" sermon.

My daughter-in-law Anita T. Smoot for transcribing my stored sermons.

My daughter Adrienne V Smoot-Edwards for writing the sermon "Christ Is Christmas," taking photographs, designing the scripture pages, and formatting the text for this publication.

The WestBow Publishing team for encouragement and all service rendered in compiling these sermonettes into book form.

To all of the above, my abiding thanks.

INTRODUCTORY THOUGHTS
FROM THE AUTHOR

When I gave the first children's sermon at my church, I was so impressed with the answers to questions I asked them that subsequent preparation and presentation of the sermons became an opportunity for my spiritual growth as well as giving the children Bible-based lessons for daily living. I tend to ramble when talking, so having a written message kept me focused when I paused to ask for input from the children. Some were given as conversations, some as stories, and some as mini lectures.

The idea to compile sermonettes for children and youth came to me as I was getting rid of several containers of stuff accumulated and kept over the years and when I was reviewing my personal papers, theater handbills, church bulletins, and an assortment of my writings for various occasions.

Years ago, I sometimes gave the sermonette to a mixed audience of children from nursery school through high school age at a designated time in the Sunday morning worship service at my church. I wanted the message to encourage them to develop a scholarly interest in reading and understanding the Bible. Many times I have heard adults, when questioned about what the Bible says or means about an issue, defer with comments like "I'm not a

Bible scholar," or "I'll leave that to the theologians." I wanted my own children to know that lessons taught in Sunday school and their daily living were based on biblical principles they can comfortably and intelligently talk about with believers or nonbelievers. Had none of the Ten Commandments been broken, there would have been no need for laws to be established by humans. Try as hard as we like, we humans will never legislate a better source than the Ten Commandments from which to learn how to live in harmony with others and enjoy life at its fullest.

When presenting these sermons to children, I used props to keep the younger children from becoming bored. Using objects to help bring clarity to the point being expressed is a lesson in itself for them. The subject matter in the sermons may be simple and short or more comprehensive, depending on the ages and maturity of the children and youth.

I share these sermons with the hope that they will inspire and incite readers of all ages to know more about life and its Creator and Sustainer, thereby making Bible study intentionally constant. Although the world is advancing in technology and science, and nations and people with differing worship styles and customs are finding themselves living side by side, the basic instructions for daily living by humankind will always be the same. Therefore, when these sermons are read, I hope the style and custom of the writer will not be a barrier to understanding the message I have tried to convey.

Be strong and very courageous. Be careful to obey all the laws my servant Moses gave you; do not turn from it to the right or to the  left that you may be successful wherever you go. Do not let this book of the law depart from your mouth; meditate on it day and night, so that you may be careful to do everything written in it. Then you will be prosperous and successful.

—Joshua 1:7–8 (NIV)

THE RELIABLE SOURCE

Good morning, children!

The Bible states in Numbers 22:18b (NKJV) "I could not go beyond the word of the Lord my God to do less or more."

I want to talk about two books. One is my favorite: the Bible; the other is a Bible directory that claims to contain five thousand facts from the scriptures.

[Holding the Bible directory] There are some very interesting things in here, but not all the information is reliable.

For instance, in one section called "General Information," it says that verse twenty-one of the seventh chapter of Ezra contains all the letters in the alphabet.

[Holding the Bible] Well, I looked it up in the reliable source, the Bible, and guess what? Twenty-five of the twenty-six letters in the alphabet are in that verse, but the most important letter of all is missing.

Ezra 7:21 [Reading from the Bible Directory]: "And I, Even I, Artaxerxes the king, issue a decree to all the treasurers who are in the region beyond the river, that what ever Ezra the priest, the scribe of the law of God of heaven may require of you,: let it be done diligently."

Which letter do you think is missing? What is our Savior's name? *Jesus*. How do we spell Jesus? The verse does not have the letter J in it. No J, no Jesus. The directory is not a reliable source.

When you study, read books, or talk with people about the Bible, remember that for all your questions, the true answers can always be found in the Bible.

God, bless our children everywhere and make them mindful that all they need to know and do to have an abundant life is recorded in your Word. In Jesus's name. Amen.

When you pass through the waters, I will be with you.

And when you pass through the rivers they will not sweep over you.

When you walk through the fire you will not be burned; the flames will not set you ablaze.

For I am the LORD, your God, the Holy One of Israel. Your Savior.

—Isaiah 43:2–3 (NLV)

UPSTREAM LIVING

Good morning, children!

Today we are going to talk about being upstream Christians in a downstream world. From the Bible we will use verse four from first John, chapter four (NIV): "You, dear children, are from God and have overcome them, because the one who is in you is greater than the one who is in the world."

Who knows what a stream is? A body of running water. Who has seen a stream? Most of us have seen the streams that flow down the street during heavy rain falls or storms. What do we see flowing down these streams? Garbage, leaves, trash, and driftwood. Do you know what driftwood is? The dictionary defines it simply as "wood that is drifted or floated by water." Where do streams from the streets lead? To the sewer. Yes, all the garbage, leaves, trash, and driftwood float straight down the stream to a sewer.

Let's get back to our Bible verse: "You, dear children, are from God and have overcome them, because the one [God] who is in you is greater than the one [Satan] who is in the world." Now we know that to talk about God and Satan together means both bad news and good news.

The bad news is that Satan is he who is in the world. The Bible tells us in several places that Satan is the prince of darkness. Just imagine him and his followers as the garbage and the driftwood floating downstream; you see, it takes no effort to go with the flow. For these folks, when they hear others using profanity, they use profanity; if others steal, they steal; if others tell untruths, they tell untruths. They will simply go with the flow, and someday they will be forever lost in the sewer of eternity: hell.

The good news is that God is king of heaven and the world. He sent his son Jesus to be Lord for those of us who receive, trust, and follow him. As his followers, we cannot go with Satan; therefore, we must go upstream—*against* the flow. We let others see Christ in us. We do not use profanity and we are honest: we never cheat on exams or tell untruths. We say grace before we eat, whether at home or in public places. Because we have Christ in us, we can say with confidence that we will not drift downstream and be lost forever. We will always go upstream and end up safe in heaven because "greater is he who is in us than he who is in the world."

Father in heaven, thank you for these children. Let them remember that following Jesus is like swimming upstream in this downstream world. We ask, in the words of Jesus as recorded in Saint John 17:15, not that you take them out of the world but that you will keep them from evil. Thank you for the parents who sent or brought them here to learn of your will for their lives. Make each adult here an island they can hold onto when the stream gets too rough for them to swim alone. Your will be done in the name of Jesus. Amen.

If my people, who are called by my name, will humble themselves and pray and seek my face 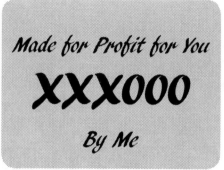 and turn from their wicked ways, then I will hear from heaven, and I will forgive their sin and will heal their land.

—2 Chronicles 7:14 (NIV)

A Designer Label:
Authentic or Imitation

Good morning, children!

Do you know what the word *authentic* means? "Genuine, trustworthy, free from hypocrisy or pretense, or *real*." Do you know what the word *imitation* means? "Counterfeit, resembles something else that is genuine, or *fake*."

We are a generation who wants our cars, household appliances, and toys to have well-known brand names. We want clothes by famous designers. We want the signature of a celebrity on things we wear. We don't need to know these folks personally, and they don't care who buys or wears their labels. Some folks will steal, borrow, rent, or buy copies or used items just to wear a designer label. Some will even kill another human being just to possess a well-known brand name or wear a designer label. I could go on and on about labels we buy—but that's another story.

Today I'm talking about a designer label that doesn't cost money. You just have to know the designer personally, and the designer has to know you. It's the Christian label. The designer is Christ. An authentic Christian label costs nothing but God's approval, yet only a few people wear it. How do we know the difference between the authentic and the imitation Christian label? The Bible tells us.

2 Timothy 2:19 (NIV) states, "Nevertheless, God's solid foundation stands firm, sealed with this inscription: 'The Lord knows those who are his,' and 'everyone who confesses the name of the Lord must turn away from wickedness.'" That's one description of the authentic Christian label. If your Christian label is authentic, you have turned from sinful ways. You love God with all your heart, and you love each other as yourself. You don't hurt each other's feelings on purpose, and you keep the Ten Commandments. Before going along with what everyone else is doing, ask yourself, What would Jesus do in this situation? To know the answer, study your Bible and ask the Lord to guide you in everything you do each day.

Many people wear an imitation Christian label because they never bother to get God's approval. You see, children, Christianity is imitation when you come to church every Sunday, sing in the choir, or do other church work just to be seen or to impress people. It is imitation when you give gifts to get gifts and when you do good things to get awards, plaques, or special favors in return. Jesus tells us what the outcome will be for those who wear an imitation Christian label. Matthew 7:21–23 (NIV) states,

> Not everyone who says to me, "Lord, Lord" will enter the kingdom of heaven, but only he that does the will of my father which is in heaven. Many will say to me on that day, "Lord, Lord, did we not prophesy in your name and in your name drive out demons and perform many miracles?" Then I will

tell them plainly, "I never knew you. Away from me, you evildoers!"

Have you ever heard someone say, "I wouldn't be caught dead in that outfit," or "I wouldn't be caught dead riding in that old car"? Well, children, if you don't want to hear the Lord say, "I never knew you; depart from me," don't be caught dead wearing an imitation Christian label. Get to know Christ the designer so he knows you as his own.

Father in heaven, we praise your name and thank you for our daily blessings, especially our children. Thank you for the privilege of being able to wear, free of charge, the authentic label designed by Christ, your Son, and let us not be tempted to call ourselves Christian without your approval and his knowledge. In Christ's name we pray. Amen.

If you love me, you will obey what I command and I will ask the Father and He will give you another Counselor to be with you forever.

—John 14:15–16 (NIV)

LIVING WITH THE SPIRIT

Good morning, children!

This year at Zion, we are studying and learning about the Holy Spirit. Every person has the freedom to choose to live by the guidance of the Holy Spirit or by the standards of Satan.

From God's Word, let's look at Galatians 5:16 (NIV). It reads, "So I Say, live by the Spirit, and you will not gratify the desires of the sinful nature." Then John 14:2 states, "In my Father's house are many rooms; ... I am going there to prepare a place for you."

To illustrate a meaning of these verses, I've made up some stories about two people who become Christians. One of them is living by the Holy Spirit and the other is gratifying the desires of the sinful nature.

The first story is about Felix. Felix is a gambler. One day he goes to his *basement* (racetrack) to get a *silver tray* (gambling habit). He hears a knock at his front door and comes upstairs, bringing the silver tray with him. When he opens the door, he finds Jesus there. He invites Jesus to come in and stay for a while, but Jesus says, "I can't stay. I have some business to take care of in my Father's house. I'm going to send you someone who can stay as long as you want him. His name is the Holy Spirit, and he can show you how to *polish* (stop gambling) that silver tray you have there. If you follow his instructions, you'll never need to polish it again."

Before Felix closes the door, the Holy Spirit walks in. Felix wants to sit down in his *living room* (church) and get acquainted with the Holy Spirit, but his *silver tray* (gambling habit) is an embarrassment. "Excuse me, Holy Spirit, I'll be right back," he says as he picks up the silver tray and hurries to the *basement* (racetrack). He is about to put the tray on a shelf when the Holy Spirit calls down and says, "Brother Felix, are you polishing that tray you took down? If so, I'd be glad to help you. Polishing silver is one of my specialties." Felix answers, "Oh no, Holy Spirit, it's too messy down here. Just make yourself comfortable there in the *living room* (church). I've got some real good polish around here somewhere. For now, I'll just take a cloth and give it a lick and a promise so it won't look too bad when I put it back in the *living room* (church). By the way, turn on the TV, please. It's almost time for them to read off today's lottery numbers." Felix is gratifying the desires of the sinful nature.

The other story is about Hosanna. Hosanna is a gossiper who has been looking for a roomer. One day, she is taking a pan full of *dirty dishes* (gossip) to her sink when she hears a knock at her door. She opens her door and finds Jesus there. Jesus says, "I'm just stopping for a minute. I can't stay. I have to leave to take care of some important business in my Father's house. I wanted to come in person to let you know I'm sending you a roomer. His name is the Holy Spirit, and he likes to keep busy." Hosanna is so excited that she leaves the door open. In a little while, the Holy Spirit walks in and they greet each other. The Holy Spirit asks to see the house, so Hosanna starts with her *kitchen* (neighborhood). Now she has always kept some *dirty dishes* (gossip) in her *kitchen* (neighborhood), but she doesn't want the Holy Spirit to know this. So she says, "Oh my! Let me *wash* (stop gossiping) these dirty dishes before we go any farther. This won't take long, Holy Spirit. You just stay here and keep me company."

She gets her *detergent* (prayer), runs some water, and starts washing dishes. The Holy Spirit quickly takes a towel and dries the dishes for her. She notices that as he dries each dish, he carefully puts it away in its proper place. Hosanna likes the way the Holy Spirit does his work so much that she thinks to herself, *Keeping this house clean is going to be easy with the Holy Spirit here to help me.* Hosanna is living by the Spirit.

Father in heaven, as we and our children learn to live by the Spirit, please make us sensitive to his presence so we may know his voice as he directs us to do your will. In the name of Jesus we pray. Amen.

I am the vine, you are the branches. If a man remains in me and I in him, he will bear much fruit; apart from me you can do nothing.

—Saint John 15:5 (NIV)

The Vine and the Branches

Good morning, children!

At prayer service last Wednesday night, Deaconess Beatrice Jones read a passage of scripture from the fifteenth chapter of Saint John (NIV). Jesus is speaking throughout the entire chapter, and in verse five he says, "I am the vine, you are the branches. If a man remains in me and I in him, he will bear much fruit; apart from me you can do nothing."

Jesus is like a tree, and we are like branches. As long as the branches are connected to the tree, they grow and bear fruit. If a branch is separated from the tree, it will no longer grow, nor will it bear fruit.

This plant (a poplar tree sprig) grew from a seed from a big poplar tree in my neighbor's yard. All year long the poplar tree is bearing its fruit. For the next several weeks, leaves will be falling; next, the seeds will shower down in little pods. It blossoms early in the spring and begins to shed pollen and petal. If a limb breaks off, the limb dies. As long as the branches are attached to that tree, they are bearing the fruit God intended them to bear.

God intended that through our connection to Jesus, just like branches to a tree, we will bear the fruit of love, joy, peace, patience, kindness, goodness, self-control, faithfulness, and gentleness.

Whatever we accomplish in life, it will mean nothing unless we stay attached to Jesus.

I'm going to tell you a true story, and I want you to remember the last part of the Bible verse I read earlier: "For without me, you can do nothing."

A few years ago, a well-known man was a United States senator. He even ran for president of the United States. One of his daughters helped him with his campaign; she was his pride and joy. That daughter became a hopeless alcoholic. While under the influence of alcohol, she fell down in an alley one night and froze to death. Her father spoke about her life and death to a reporter, and a newspaper printed this quote from him: "My whole life's been gambled on the thesis that through education and information and political action, you can change things for the better."

What was wrong with his thesis? Jesus is not in it. Remember that for your accomplishments to turn out for the good, you need Jesus in whatever you do. All good things come from God.

 Father in heaven, thank you for today and for these precious branches, our children. Please keep them from falling prey to the pruning knife of Satan and help them to grow strong and bear fruit through the aid of the Holy Spirit. In Jesus's name we pray. Amen.

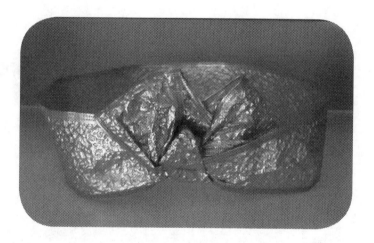

You will be a crown of splendor in the Lords hand, a royal diadem in the hand of your God.

—Isaiah 62:3 (NKJV)

CROWNS

Good morning, children!

Let's begin with prayer:

Father in heaven, I thank you for this day, these children, and the opportunity to talk with our children's children. Please make the message meaningful and make it a blessing to every listening ear. In the name of Jesus, our Lord I pray. Amen.

Our scripture for the message is Proverbs 17:6: "Children's children are the crown of old men, and the glory of the children is their father" (NKJV).

The Bible tells us that you are the crown of your grandparents. What is a crown? A crown is usually a jeweled, ornamental headdress. It is worn as a sign of honor, victory, reward, or power. It sparkles and shines at all times.

As the crown of your grandparents, you shine and sparkle when you show them love and respect, when you open doors for them, and when you say please when you ask them for something and

27

thank you when they give you something or do things for you. You should telephone and visit them often.

Crowns have to be polished in order to shine. Your grandparents polish you in two ways. One, they give you good gifts, such as love, clothes, toys, and healthy food and snacks that taste good to you. Two, they give you food for your soul. That is food that is good for you even when you do not like it. It's food for your soul when your grandparents teach you good manners, punish you when you have misbehaved, and teach you the difference between right and wrong. Best of all, they tell you about Jesus and how to live a happy life on earth and to prepare for an eternal life in heaven.

Now children, face the congregation and say together, "HAPPY GRANDPARENTS DAY!"

Weeping may remain for a night, but rejoicing comes in the morning.

—Psalm 30:5 (NIV)

CRYING AND REJOICING

Good morning, children!

What is the shortest verse in the Bible? "Jesus wept" (John 11:35 NKJV).

When Jesus lived as a human being on earth, he had a close friend named Lazarus. One day, Jesus was told that Lazarus had died. When they showed Jesus where Lazarus was buried, Jesus cried. Why did Jesus cry? Was he just showing his human side? Was he sad because Lazarus died when Jesus was not with him? Was he crying tears of joy? After all, he knew before Lazarus died that Jesus was going to raise him up again. In John 11:11b (NKJV), Jesus said, "Our friend Lazarus sleeps, but I go that I may wake him up."

Maybe Jesus cried for all these reasons, I don't know. I do know that because the verse is so short, everybody who reads it or hears it remembers that Jesus wept.

Guess what? There is another short verse in the Bible, and like John 11:35 (NKJV), it has just two words. Jesus wants us to do what it says; that is "Rejoice always" (1 Thessalonians 5:16 NKJV).

We should rejoice always because Jesus cried, Jesus suffered, and Jesus died so we don't have to. When troubles come and we cry, it's temporary. We know that joy comes later. All we have to do is remember that Jesus wept so we can rejoice always.

 Father in heaven, thank you for loving us and for sending your Son, Jesus, from heaven to become human, homeless, hated, hurt to the point of tears, and hung on a cross so we can rejoice at all times. Protect our children, and guide us as we teach them to live in this world and to trust and serve you. In the name of Jesus I pray. Amen.

BREAKING NEWS!!

Jesus Christ Is Alive

Followers of Jesus Christ of Nazareth believe that he is alive.

This report just in … At sunrise today, three women, reported to be friends of Jesus Christ of Nazareth, went to his grave to anoint his body. However, the body was not there.

According to an obituary printed in the *Daily Herald* yesterday, Jesus was crucified and died this past Friday. His body was placed in a tomb cut in a rock. The tomb was sealed with a heavy stone and guarded by armed Roman soldiers.

The three women were overheard by a reliable source telling Jesus's apostles that as they approached the tomb, they found the stone rolled from the door of the empty tomb. Two men appeared and reminded them that Jesus had said he would be crucified but would rise on the third day.

A search of the tomb and surrounding area shows no sign of theft or any trace of the dead body of Jesus. Folks are now wondering if Jesus of Nazareth was indeed the Son of God and has in fact risen from his grave.

We will continue to follow this story as more information becomes available to us. Stay tuned to this station.

(Each child is given a copy of the obituary and the breaking news story as they sing "Jesus Loves Me" together.)

BREAKING NEWS

Good morning, children!

Let's begin with prayer.

Father in heaven, we thank you for today and for your love, mercy, and grace. Thank you for these children and youth and for the loved ones who have gathered to worship you. Most of all, we thank you for our Savior, in whose name we pray. Amen.

Today we are celebrating Palm Sunday. Next Sunday we will celebrate Easter Sunday. Can you tell me what happened between Palm Sunday and Easter Sunday morning two thousand and eight years ago?

Jesus predicted the events of that week in Matthew 2:18–19:

> Behold we are going up to Jerusalem, and the Son of Man will be betrayed to the priest and scribes; and they will condemn Him to death, and deliver Him to the Gentiles to mock and scourge and to crucify. And the third day He will rise again. (NKJV)

I wrote an obituary that includes some highlights of some of the things that happened the week before the first Easter Sunday morning. I also prepared an imaginary news broadcast account of Jesus's resurrection.

Just imagine today as the Saturday after the first Palm Sunday as I read the obituary.

Your assignment is to read the obituary again this coming Saturday and to read the "Breaking News" story next Sunday before you come to Sunday school.

The Daily Herald

Saturday March 15, 0034

Obituaries

Jesus Christ

Jesus Christ, son of Joseph and Mary of Nazareth, died yesterday at Mount Calvary, known as Golgotha, Place of the Skull. He was thirty-three years old and had no fixed address. Had he lived, this coming December would mark thirty-four years since his birth in a stable in Bethlehem. Rumors about who he was started on the night he was born when it was reported that there was a star in the eastern sky shining so bright that three kings followed it for many miles to worship and bring him gifts of gold, frankincense, and myrrh because they believed he was the Messiah the Jewish prophets predicted would come to deliver them from bondage. His death was caused by loss of blood due to a torturous crucifixion. Two unidentified thieves were put to death beside him.

Jesus grew up in Nazareth. At age twelve, he is reported to have impressed some Jewish religious leaders with his knowledge of their scriptures, and when asked about it, he claimed to be about his father's business. Three years ago, he began to preach and perform miracles. He has been known to give blind men sight, heal the sick, cast demons out of humans and swine, and feed multitudes of people by causing small amounts of food to multiply. He was often at odds with the Pharisees about breaking their rules for worship and the activities that take place in the temple.

He had twelve apostles and hundreds of followers, and wherever he went, crowds would gather to hear him preach and teach. He was well known for using parables to describe the kingdom of God. He came to town last Sunday riding on a donkey, and the crowd cheered him as Jesus, prophet from Nazareth in Galilee. He went to the temple and drove out the men who were selling doves for sacrificial offering, reminding them that the temple was a house of prayer. Afterward, he healed the blind and lame who came to the temple. When children shouted, "Hosanna to the son of David," the priests and teachers were appalled. The next day, he continued preaching and teaching and asserting that his kingdom was not of this world. The Sanhedrin, fearing reprisal from Governor Pontius Pilate, accused Jesus of breaking temple rules and disrespecting Roman authority and claiming to be the Son of God. Judas Iscariot, one of his apostles, betrayed him for an undisclosed amount of silver coins. He was arrested Thursday by Roman soldiers and tried before Governor Pilate, who declared him innocent of any crime but ordered his crucifixion because, when asked, the same crowd that praised him last Sunday chose to have the notorious criminal, Barabbas, freed instead of Jesus.

His body was removed from the cross yesterday by Arimathea and placed in a new tomb cut in a rock. The Pharisees requested that guards be placed at the grave to keep his followers from stealing his body. Survivors include his devout mother Mary, his apostles, and hundreds of followers.

(After reading the obituary, the children are given copies of the obituary and the "Breaking News" story as they sing "Jesus Loves Me.")

Psalm 23 (NIV)

The Lord Is My Shepherd,
I shall not be in want.

He makes me to lie down in green pastures

He leads me beside quiet waters,
he restores my soul.

He guides me in paths of
righteousness for his name's sake

Even though I walk through the
valley of the shadow of death

I will fear no evil, for you are with me

Your rod and your staff, they comfort me.

You prepare a table before me in
the presence of my enemies

You anoint my head with oil; my cup overflows

Surely goodness and love will
follow me all the days of my life

And I will dwell in the house
of the Lord forever.

SHEEPFOLDS

Good morning, children!

Today we are going to talk about sheepfolds. We are told in the Bible book of Isaiah 40:11 (NIV): "He tends His flock like a shepherd; He gathers the lambs with His arms and carries them close to his heart; he gently leads those that have young." There are a lot of references throughout the Bible where God refers to himself as shepherd and to humankind as sheep. To understand why, we need to know something about sheep and why they need a shepherd to survive, as well as why humans need God for their souls to survive.

The person who takes care of flocks of those hairy animals from which we get lamb chops and woolen clothes is called a shepherd, and the flocks are called sheepfolds. The sheep are completely dependent upon the shepherd for food, care, and protection. Sheep do not swim and so will drown if they lose footing even in shallow water. The mother sheep does not recognize her baby lamb and will neglect to feed her own, and if a sheep strays from the flock, it cannot find its way back alone. Sheep are totally dependent upon the shepherd.

When searching for information regarding sheep, I paraphrased the following summary of facts from the Britannica encyclopedia:

Shepherds feed their sheep an abundance of grass or grazing fodder found in pastures. Sheep need a diet of choice grass mixed with course brushy materials and weeds. During the winter and in periods of drought they are fed hay, roughage and small amounts of grain. A sheep needs up to 1 ½ gallons of water daily. They must graze no more than three or four miles between the grazing location and their water source and less depending upon the age of lambs. The shepherd must monitor the births of the lambs to make certain the ewe (mother) recognizes her lamb and allows it to nurse. The shepherd must make sure the lamb does not get cold after its birth. For skilled care, a shepherd manages small flocks of ten to one hundred sheep. He uses sheep dogs to guard, guide and tend the sheep. Small bells are placed around the necks of the mature and stable sheep. The young and straying sheep are less likely to scatter or stray very far from the sound of the bell sheep.

Here at church, for us to grow and develop a Christlike lifestyle, we must be like sheep. God is our shepherd, and our pastor is the under-shepherd through whom God feeds and nurtures the congregation (sheep, lambs, and the unborn/unsaved). God tells his under-shepherd in 1 Peter 5:2–3 (NIV) "Be Shepherds of God's flock that is under your care, serving as overseers, not because you must, but because you are willing, as God wants you to be, not greedy for money but eager to serve; not lording it over those entrusted to you but being examples to the flock." God tells the church members in Psalm 100:3 (NIV): "Know that the Lord is God. It is He who made us and we are His; we are His people and the sheep of his pasture."

Jesus tells the under-shepherd in John 21:17 to "Feed my sheep." Our food comes from the Bible. It is the Word of God, as described in Hebrews 4:12 (NIV): "For the word of God is living and active. Sharper than any double-edged sword, it penetrates even to dividing soul and spirit, joints and marrow; it judges the thoughts and attitudes of the heart." And in John 6:35 (NIV): "Then Jesus declared, I am the bread of life. He who comes to me will never go hungry and he who believes in me will never be thirsty."

So, children, if we compare our church family's care and management with the care and management of sheep, we get an idea of why David said in Psalm 23 that the Lord is our shepherd, we shall not want because the Lord makes us lie down in green pastures. He leads us beside still waters and, among other things, the Lord leads us in the paths of righteous living. It is the responsibility of our under-shepherd, the pastor, to feed us the bread of life and to nurture us with counsel and instruction in ways to care for the lambs (new disciples) and the unborn (persons who have not accepted Jesus as Lord and become baptized believers). The deacons/sheepfold leaders (sheep dogs) are responsible for making sure there is nothing in the way of you getting food, guarding you against satanic intrusions, comforting you when you face challenges, and encouraging you to eat a proper bread-of-life diet. The seasoned saints and clergy (bell sheep) are responsible to be the church family mentors who make the church a lighthouse for you to find your way to where the bread of life is given.

One way to understand the difference between the soul food humans eat and the food that sheep eat is by substituting the sheep diet for a made-up bread-of-life diet for the church family. For example:

Roughage becomes submission to the leadership of the under-shepherd.

Choice grass becomes music, CME (Christmas, Mothers Day, and Easter) worship services, fellowship and anniversary celebrations.

Weeds become Bible study, Sunday school, and ministry participation.

Grain becomes revivals and regular church attendance.

Hay becomes ministry to prisoners, visitation to sick/housebound, and community outreach.

Water becomes constant exposure and participation in all of the above.

 Father in heaven, thank you for sending your Son, Jesus, to be our Good Shepherd. Forgive us for our tendency to stray. Lead us to pastures of righteous living, and fill us with the bread of life. Guide us to take care of our lambs and unborn. Through Jesus the Good Shepherd we pray. Amen.

Consider how the lilies grow. They do not labor or spin. Yet I tell you, not even Solomon in all his splendor was dressed like one of these

—*Luke 12:27 (NIV)*

We remember the fish we ate in Egypt at no cost—also the cucumbers, melons, leeks, onions and garlic.

—*Numbers 11:5 (NIV)*

ONIONS AND LILIES

Good morning, children!

If you look around in the church, you see the choir, the ushers, the pastor and his assistants, and the congregation. If you are in Sunday school, you have teachers and others who teach you knowledge and understanding of the Bible and how to use your talents to serve others. The members in our church family do not all have the same gift, but when we assemble together, we use our different gifts to make us one whole body in worship and ministry. Yes, children, we're all in the same family, and we must learn to use our individual gifts as best we can to keep the whole church body growing and healthy.

Today I'm going to talk about the lily, a flower, and the onion, a vegetable, to help you understand how different something or someone can be and still belong to the same family.

In Luke 12:27 (NIV) Jesus says, "Consider how the lilies grow. They do not labor or spin. Yet I tell you, not even Solomon in all his splendor was dressed like one of these." Consider the lilies. Children, do you know that the onion is a member of the lily family?

The lilies that bloom and the onions we eat are both members of the liliaceae plant family. There are white, red, purple, and gold lilies. We call some daylilies and some wild lilies of the field. The white lily we see at Easter was known as the plant of purity in the nineteenth century. The flower has a trumpet shape and a fragrance that is nothing like the onion. Just as there are many different kinds of lilies, there are different kinds of onions. There are Bermuda, Vidalia, red, green, and yellow onions we use as vegetables in soup, stews, salads, and sandwiches.

The onion does not smell like the flower. It has no eye-appealing beauty and often drives us to tears, but if you want a beef stew to taste good, you put some onions in it. If you want a beautiful, sweet-smelling centerpiece for the dining room table, you use the Easter lily.

Members of the church family must be able to use our various gifts to prepare the church as a dining room for serving God and his people generous helpings of the fruit of the Spirit that taste good in an atmosphere with a sweet-smelling aroma. In fact, we are told in 1 Corinthians 12:4 (NIV), "There are different kinds of gifts, but the same spirit. There are different kinds of service but the same Lord. There are different kinds of workings but the same God works all of them in men."

You see, children, we often try so hard to look and smell like the lily that we become upset with others around us who have the onion characteristics needed to nourish and provide us with what we need to have a healthy church body. As you grow in faith and knowledge of your spiritual gifts, you will be able to understand that we must not allow our differences to divide us and keep us from becoming one in spirit as a church family. Remember, children, God loves and cares as much for the onion as he does the lily, and he gets as much glory from the one that smells bad and has no outward beauty as he does from the one that smells good and has eye-appealing beauty.

The melodious and inspiring voices you hear coming from the choir, the guidance of the ushers to help you find your way and feel welcome in this building, the lessons taught from the Bible by Sunday school teachers, the sermons preached by our pastor, and the scolding by your parents and other adults when you misbehave are all different gifts used to help you to grow and use your gift as God intended.

 Father in heaven, thank you for our different gifts that make it impossible for us to be complete without working them all together. Forgive us for using our gifts in ways that hurt one another and bring displeasure to you. Help each one of us to use our gift to its fullest potential in building your kingdom on earth. Thank you for the cornerstone Jesus, in whose name we pray. Amen.

We Must Build a Holy Temple

(Written by Bertha Smoot)

(Tune: Battle Hymn of the Republic)

In obedience to the Father, at Calvary
Christ died / So every race and nation,
through his blood, be purified. / We're to
build a holy temple in one body unified /
Where God's Spirit lives.

We must build a holy temple / We must
build a holy temple / We must build a holy
temple / Where God's Spirit lives.

Not with bricks and mortar but with living
stones, my brother, / With a foundation
on the prophets, apostles, and none other /
Than Jesus as chief cornerstone; our talents
as the builder / Of a dwelling place for love.

We must build a holy temple / We must
build a holy temple / We must build a holy
temple / Where God's Spirit lives.

BUILDING A HOLY TEMPLE

Good morning, children!

Today we are going to talk about building the church. What is the church? Is it a building with walls, windows, floors, and a roof? How do we build the church? Is the church a building or a household of individuals? We find the answers in Ephesians 2:19–22 (NIV):

> Consequently, you are no longer foreigners and aliens, but fellow citizens with God's people and members of God's household, built on the foundation of the apostles and prophets, with Christ Jesus himself as the chief cornerstone. In Him the whole building is joined together and rises to become a holy temple in the Lord. And in Him you are being built together to become a dwelling in which God lives by his Spirit.

Paul the Apostle is telling the household of believers at Ephesus that everyone who believes that Jesus is the Son of God, shed his blood and died for the atonement of sin, and arose from death to life eternal is adopted into one household. All who believe, regardless of race or nationality, are fellow citizens with the saints and members of the same household.

This building process reaches the projected outcome when Jews and Gentiles become reconciled through Christ Jesus for the purpose of completing a dwelling place for God. According to 1 Peter 2:5 (NIV), "You also, like living stones, are being built into a spiritual house to be a holy priesthood, offering spiritual sacrifices acceptable to God through Jesus Christ."

This building where we come to worship, learn about God, and fellowship with one another is not where God's Spirit lives. This building is a physical structure. The church we are talking about today is a body of believers constantly growing in unity of spirit.

I close today's talk by sharing the lesson in a couple of verses I wrote for you to sing.

So, in the tune of the "Battle Hymn of the Republic," please sing "We Must Build a Holy Temple."

Father in heaven, we thank you for adopting us into your household. Keep us forever focused on building a temple fit for your Spirit to dwell. Through Christ, the chief cornerstone, we pray. Amen.

Give us, Lord, a bit o' sun,
A bit o' work and a bit o' fun,
Give us in all the struggle and sputter,
Our daily bread and a bit o' butter,
Give us health our keep to make
And a bit to spare for other's sake
Give us, too, a bit of song,
And a tale and a book to help us along,
Give us, Lord, a chance to be
Our goodly best, brave, wise, and free,
Our goodly best for ourselves and others
Till all men learn to live as brothers.

An Old English Prayer
Author Unknown

GIVING THANKS BEFORE MEALS

Good morning, children!

Today we are going to talk about giving thanks before we eat. We call it "blessing our food" or "saying grace" at mealtime. For believers, it is to give God glory by thanking him for providing the food before us and asking him to bless it; thereby insuring that it nourishes us and does no harm to our bodies.

In 1 Corinthians 10: 31(NIV), Paul the Apostle writes, "So whether you eat or drink or whatever you do, do it all for the glory of God."

Through the ages, believers of different nations and customs have adopted traditional ways of thanking God for and asking him to bless what we eat. Because of cultural or health beliefs about the food we eat, this scripture reminds us that God is the source from which all food comes; therefore, when food is provided to assuage our hunger, no harm comes to our bodies if we eat it with thanksgiving to the source from which it comes.

As Baptists, we do not subscribe to a standard wording for giving thanks and asking a blessing for our food. However, I am going to share four traditional blessings you might have heard.

Protestant: "Bless, O Lord, this food to our use, and us to Thy services, and make us ever mindful of the needs of others, in Jesus Name, Amen."

Jewish: "Lift up your hands toward the sanctuary and bless the Lord. Blessed art Thou, O Lord our God, King of the universe, who brings forth bread for the earth. Amen."

Roman Catholic: "Bless us, O Lord, and these Thy gifts which we are about to receive from Thy bounty. Through Christ our Lord. Amen."

Eastern Orthodox: "The Hungry shall eat and shall be satisfied, and those who seek out the Lord shall praise Him; their hearts shall live forever. Glory to the Father and to the Son, and to the Holy Ghost, both now and ever, and unto ages of ages. Amen."

A familiar child's blessing: "God is great, God is good, and we thank Him for our food. By His hands we all are fed; give us, Lord, our daily bread. Amen."

Father, thank you for the opportunity to remind our children that thanking you before we eat gives you glory, and in so doing, we ask and receive your blessing on whatever food is before us. Through Christ our Lord we pray. Amen.

Teach Me

Teach me, O Lord, to be sweet and gentle. In all the events of life; in disappointments, in the thoughtlessness of others, in the insincerity of those I trusted, in the unfaithfulness of those on whom I relied. Teach me to profit by the suffering that comes across my path. May no one be less good for having. Come within my influence; no one less pure, less true, less kind, less noble for having been a fellow-traveler in our journey toward Eternal life.

—Author Unknown

Why do you look at the speck of sawdust in your brother's eye and pay no attention to the plank in your own eye? ... You hypocrite, first take the plank out of your eye, and then you will see clearly to remove the speck from your brother's eye.

—Luke 6:41–42

JONAH MOMENTS

Good morning, children!

Today we are going to talk about anger and compassion. Why do we become angry when others are not punished for doing something wrong? Why is it hard for us to help someone who we feel is undeserving? Why should we be compassionate? When do we show compassion? The answers to the questions are not easy. The book of Jonah in the Bible is about the prophet Jonah's anger and God's compassion. I want you to read or ask your parents to read the book of Jonah to you. It is a short book of four chapters. Today's talk is from chapter 4:1–2, 4 in the New International Version of the Bible.

> But Jonah was greatly displeased and became angry. He prayed to the Lord, "O Lord, is this not what I said when I was still at home? That is why I was so quick to flee to Tarshish. I knew that you are a gracious and compassionate God, slow to anger and abounding in love, a God who relents from sending calamity." But the Lord replied, "Have you any right to be angry?"

When you read or have someone read to you the entire book of Jonah, you will learn that as a minor prophet, God chose Jonah to warn wicked people in the city of Nineveh that it would be destroyed unless they repented and turned from their wicked living. Jonah did not feel that the city should be spared, so he ran away and boarded a ship sailing to Tarshish. He was thrown overboard and swallowed by a big fish that vomited him up on dry land after three days. He finally went to Nineveh and preached as God had told him. The people repented, and the city was spared. Jonah was not happy and had a pity party, questioning God about his mercy on Nineveh. God reminds Jonah that God had shown him the same compassion. When Jonah disobeyed God, his life was spared, and when he needed shade from the sun, a tree was provided.

We, too, have Jonah moments sometimes. One of my Jonah moments resulted after I gave the visitors' welcome at church and asked our members to stand and greet one another. This resulted in what I felt was a happy hour that had no place in a church service. I was disappointed with the pastor for allowing it to continue. When a member's family requested a meet-and-greet welcome at his funeral because it was one of his favorite parts of the worship experience, I began to feel better. Now when I look around the sanctuary and see the smiles, hugs, and handshakes, I understand the meet-and-greet fellowship's relevance in the service. While I was displeased and felt that the extended time we were spending greeting one another was taking away from praise and worship of the Lord, I was forgetting the glory the Lord gets when we show love and kindness to one another.

When you are asked to share your toys with someone who has broken his own, does it upset you? When you and your friends misbehave and they get to play outside but your parents keep you inside as punishment, do you want your friends to be punished too? If your answers are yes, those were Jonah moments. The next time you are about to have a Jonah moment, try to remember when you were not punished for misbehaving. You see, children, we all receive compassion we do not deserve. It is called God's grace, and neither Jonah nor we have the right to be angry when others are shown compassion in spite of their sins.

Dear Lord, when we become angry at others for their transgressions, remind us that we, too, are transgressors at times. Forgive us and give us the courage to forgive them. Thank you for your enduring compassion toward all of us. We pray in Jesus's name. Amen.

We also engage to maintain family and secret devotions; to study diligently the word of God and to religiously educate our children.

—Excerpt from Church Covenant

OUR CHURCH COVENANT

Good morning, children!

Today is Diaconate Sunday. It is the fourth anniversary of the ordination of deaconesses and the official establishment of our diaconate team ministry here at Zion. One of the most important roles of a diaconate team is to encourage and empower our families in Zion as we strive together to become better Christians and learn to love and trust God above anyone and anything else.

So my talk today is about families and what the Bible and our church covenant say about how your parents should raise you. The Bible says in Deuteronomy 6:5–7 (NIV),

> Love the Lord your God with all your heart, and with all your soul and with all your strength. These commandments that I give you today are to be upon your hearts. Impress them on your children. Talk about them when you sit at home and when you walk along the road, when you lie down and when you get up.

And from our church covenant, your parents promise to religiously educate you and to have family devotion.

Now, children, when your parents send or bring you to Sunday school, whether you want to come or not, remember they made a promise that they would religiously educate you. Do your parents have a special time when they sit down with you and share in Bible reading, prayer, and other ways to give thanks and show God that you love him? If they do, that's called devotion. Even though this happens when you would rather play, remember they are following the rules that they have promised God and their church family they would follow.

Heavenly Father, your love and mercy never fail us. Please help us in return to be faithful in bringing up these children as your Word directs and as we promise through covenant to do. Thank you for our children and the privilege of having you as our Father. In the name of Jesus. Amen.

Is there no balm in Gilead? Is there no physician there? Why then is there no healing for the wound of my people?

—Jeremiah 8:22 (NIV)

We hoped for peace but no good has come for a time of healing.

—Jeremiah 8:15

Booster Shots

Good morning, children!

Today is Deaconess Day here at Zion. You have seen the deaconesses helping with baptism and with communion. You might also know that, among other things, they visit the sick and assist with the church's outreach ministry to people in need of food, clothes, and shelter. Some of you who have been attending Sunday school should know that Paul the Apostle tells us that the deaconess is a servant of the church. I wanted to tell you something you might not know about the deaconess, so I did some research.

Who knows who Florence Nightingale was? (She is considered the founder of modern nursing.) Well, during my research I learned that in the nineteenth century, the main function of the deaconess was nursing. In fact, Florence Nightingale did her practice nursing with deaconesses. Today, unless a deaconess happens to be a trained nurse or other medical specialist, she no longer takes care of the health needs of our bodies. Today, health care providers must be trained and licensed. Thanks to mankind's progress in science and technology, we have all kinds of gadgets and machines for healing the body and freedom from manual labor. We have a variety of forms of entertainment for our amusement. Our bodies are in good hands, but some of the things that bring healing, comfort, and amusement have surrounded us with hundreds of germs that are causing an epidemic of soul neglect.

Just as a syringe supplies medication for the health of our bodies, the Bible supplies medication for the health of our souls. In spite of everything we do for our bodies, they will die. Eternal life is promised only for our souls. When we accept Jesus as our personal Savior, we receive a vaccination that prevents the death of our souls. In order to build immunity against the germs I mentioned, we must take booster shots. The booster shots we are talking about today contain medicine to keep you healthy. For example, let's talk about just four germs that cause us to neglect our souls and the booster shots that guard against them.

1) Peer Pressure: You do something wrong because you don't want to be called chicken. Ephesians 5:6–7 (NIV) says, "Let no one deceive you with empty words, for because of such things God's wrath comes on those who are disobedient. Therefore do not be partners with them." Don't be afraid of being called a chicken for doing the right thing.

2) Status Symbols: You want something just because someone else has it. Exodus 20:17 (NIV) says, "You shall not covet anything that is thy neighbor's." Classmates have the newest game systems that are popular. So you pressure your parents to purchase one for you. You feel ashamed to wear your old jacket because your friends have new ones and they tease you. Remember that you are as warm in the old jacket as your friends are in their new ones. Perhaps

your parents do not have money enough to buy expensive toys.

3) Individual Rights (freedom from discipline): You do whatever you want without fear of discipline. I once heard a preacher say, "Freedom from discipline is a destructive device, designed by the devil, to deprive man of a divine destiny." Your parents discipline you because they love you and don't want you to do something that may be harmful to you. In Revelations 3:19 (NIV) God says, "Those whom I love I rebuke and discipline."

4) Denial: For people of color here in America, there is the denial of who we are. Every decade or so, we rename ourselves. When I was your age, we were colored; when I was in college, we were Negroes; when I was your mother's age, we were Black; and since I've become a senior citizen, we are African Americans. Galatians 4:31 (NIV) states, "Therefore brothers we are not children of the slave woman, but of the free woman. It is for freedom that Christ has set us free. Stand firm then and do not let yourselves be burdened again by a yoke of slavery." Remember that our freedom is not based on what others or we call us.

You are probably wondering what nurses, germs, and booster shots have to do with the deaconess. Well, a nurse applies TLC (tender loving care) for the health and care of our bodies. The nurse uses medical knowledge and skill when she or he takes a syringe and gives us a shot. As a servant in the church, a deaconess is a spiritual nurse who applies JLYC ("Jesus loves you" care) for the health of the soul. She uses kind words and good deeds to make sure the members of her church family get their booster shots.

(The deaconesses hug the children.)

Father in heaven, thank you for these children, and thank you for this opportunity for the deaconesses to demonstrate through these hugs that we love them. Bless their parents and the homes represented by their presence here. Bless this deaconess board. Enrich our minds with wisdom, and inspire our hearts with willingness to carry out the ministry that our church family has entrusted to us according to your will. Through Jesus we pray. Amen.

Let your Light shine before men, that they may see your good deeds and praise your Father in heaven.

— Matthew 5:16 (NIV)

The Shoe Shine

(Joel V. Smoot, Sr., Author)

Good morning, boys and girls.

Today I have with me two boots. As you can see, one of them is shiny and one of them is not. The one that shines is an older boot, and the one that doesn't is a brand-new boot. The older boot has been broken in. It's been worn many, many times, it's been put through the mud, it's been used for days and days, it's been worked hard and been proven to be a really good boot. It's been polished many, many times, it's comfortable to wear, and it shines brightly from every angle you see it. The older boot is ready for inspection, and the newer boot is not. Don't get me wrong; the new boot is nice. It's good, it even smells fresh and new. It just hasn't been polished yet. It hasn't been tested through the mud and hard work yet. But it will get its chance to shine.

You see, children, in a way you are all just like this new boot. You are fresh out of the box, and you look great, but you haven't been tested, you haven't been put through the mud that life can bring. But if you're polished, you'll always be ready for inspection. You see, as Christians we always have to be ready to present ourselves ready for inspection. The world is full of people who need to see our example. That's why you have to shine as bright as you can at all times and from every angle. You have to do your very best in all things. You have to obey your parents without delay or distraction. That's what God means in his commandment to "Honor thy father and mother." You have to focus and pay attention in school. Work hard and get the best grades you can. You have to be a good friend and be honest and kind. These things will put you on your way to a really good shine, a good start. But you still won't be ready for inspection; you won't shine from every angle until you're ready for God's inspection. The way to be ready for God's inspection comes in three simple steps.

Step One: Get the right polish.

The right polish is the polish that Jesus gave us when he died for our sins on the cross. This is the only polish that will give you an "inspection ready" shine. Sure there are other polishes out there, but this is the only one that is filled with God's love. It's been based in the blood of Christ Jesus, and it shines from every possible angle. No other shine will do if you want to pass God's inspection. So you have to accept Christ Jesus as your Lord and Savior. No other "savior" will do. No amount of money, knowledge, or science, no acts of kindness will get you through God's inspection. Only the blood of Jesus will help you pass God's inspection.

Step Two: Get the right instructions.

The right instructions are only found in God's Word. You'll find a whole lot of them really easy in the Holy Bible. Sure, there are a lot of other books out there that have some good things to say, and it's good to be familiar with how other people feel, but the only place a Christian has to look is right here in God's instruction manual. Another good way to get good instructions is to pray to God for wisdom. Prayer is one good way to get the instructions you need directly from the Source. Sit still and listen closely, and when God is ready he'll speak to your heart. You'll know it's his voice when you pay very close attention to what others are saying and doing. God speaks to us quite often through other people and will give signs that only you'll see. When you hear or see the same thing a few times after you've prayed for wisdom, you'll know in your heart it's an instruction from God. Follow his instructions and you'll know what you'll have to do to shine in any situation.

Step Three: Apply the Holy Spirit.

The Holy Spirit comes to you when you've accepted Jesus Christ as your Savior and have been baptized. It gives us the power we need to overcome any obstacle the world can throw at us. The Holy Spirit is God's presence here on earth. It moves through everything and is everywhere. Open your heart to it, and it will guide you through God's instructions. Do as it leads you, and God will use you to do his work here on earth, and you will be a blessing to others and spread God's love through the world. The Holy Spirit is what gives you the extra glow no human effort can. That's the shine.

Heavenly Father, as your Son's blood makes us worthy of salvation, let your Holy Spirit be the "boots" for our daily walk. Give us the strength and courage to keep them shining for the world to see him in us. This we ask in his name. Amen.

If anyone has material possessions and sees his brother in need but has no pity on him, how can the love of God be in him? Dear children let us not love with words or tongue but with actions and in truth.

—1 John 3:17–18 (NIV)

Then Mary took an expensive perfume; she poured it on Jesus' feet and wiped his feet with her hair ... You will always have the poor among you.

—John 12:3 (NIV)

A Kingdom Building Conflict

Setting: A meeting of the church congregation

Cast: Narrator, Trustee Ministry Chair, Project Committee Coordinator, PC Member, and Members 1, 2, and 3

Narrator: Today's meeting has been called for the purpose of discussing two projects that have been recommended by the Trustee Ministry; however, members of the congregation are concerned that doing both projects is too costly and have become divided and want to vote, some for one and some for the other. One project is to replace the old windows with brighter, multicolored stained-glass ones. The other project is to open a soup kitchen to serve at least one meal daily for those who are in need of food. Following the discussion, the congregation must decide which project the majority will support. The discussion begins.

Trustee Ministry Chair (rising): Brothers and sisters, as you know, the lighting in the church will be greatly improved by replacing the old windows with brighter ones that reflect light and depict the story of our Christian beliefs. You also know that a soup kitchen will help feed the hungry here and in our community, and it is our Christian duty to provide food for the hungry. In our talking with you, we found that most of you would like to do both. You have elected us as watchmen over this church, and according to Isaiah 52:8, the watchmen must lift their voices in song together, and in so doing, they can see eye to eye. We understand your concerns, and after prayer and much thought, we believe that both projects can be done if we maintain our unity of spirit. (He or she yields the floor to the Project Committee (PC) Coordinator.)

PC Coordinator (coming forward): For those among you whose hearts' desire is to glorify God by beautifying the church with new windows that will enhance lighting and reflect the gospel story, and that is what the Holy Spirit is leading you to do, there is no reason for you to criticize and oppose others who do not feel the way you do. Remember the woman who poured expensive perfume on the feet of Jesus? He didn't condemn her. He said she had done well and told the disciples that the poor will always be with us.

Member 1 (raises hand): You know, I hadn't thought about what the Bible says. I have been in this church a long time, and I love it, and I love the Lord. The new window would beautify the edifice and provide better lighting, and I believe God would be pleased if we honor him that way. I plan to pay for a window so that future generations will see my name on the plaque beneath that window and know that I contributed to making this a place to worship in beauty and holiness. We can do the windows now and start a soup kitchen later.

Member 2 (rising): On the other hand, I believe feeding hungry people should come first. Remember the rich man who Jesus told to sell what he had and distribute the proceeds to the poor? I want my contribution to be used to open the soup kitchen. I—

Member 1 (interrupting): I plan to support both projects. When you put it to a vote, why not add a third choice for those of us who will contribute to both projects? It might stop the bickering, and both projects can begin to move forward.

Member 3 (standing): I don't plan to vote at all. I'm going to contribute as much as I can on faith. To argue about or refuse to support a project because it is not my personal choice would be wrong. I intend to contribute so the mission of the church can be accomplished. If you leaders use the money for any other purpose, you will be held accountable.

PC Coordinator (rises): Amen, Brother/Sister _____. Before we vote and adjourn, I would like to thank the congregation for your support and confidence in our leadership. If our church is to triumph, we leaders need you to pray for us to stay rooted and grounded in the Word and diligent in our service as overseers of this church so we not be compulsive, unwilling, or dishonest in the performance of our duties.

PC Member (getting the attention of PC Coordinator): Please don't forget to remind them about Tuesday night's Prayer and Praise service for the success of our ministry efforts.

Narrator (as the vote is about to begin): Due to time constraints, we must end our coverage of tonight's meeting. We urge you to read Hebrews 13:7, 17 for a clearer understanding of how sacrificial offerings are given by members and the responsibility of our leaders as good stewards of the offerings entrusted to them. For more about the woman who poured perfume on the feet of Jesus, read Luke 7:36–50, and about the rich man, read Luke 18:18–22.

Everyone who believes that Jesus is the
Christ is born of God and everyone who
loves the Father loves His Child as well.

—1 John 5:1

Merry Christmas

CHRIST IS CHRISTMAS
(Adrienne V. Smoot-Edwards, Author)

(Use chalkboard for prop.)

Good morning, children!

Who knows what an abbreviation is? An abbreviation is a way to shortcut what you are writing using a kind of language that everyone understands. Abbreviations are common and are used daily in written communications. For example, if I write (write "Mon." on chalkboard), what does it mean? Monday. Does it change the day of the week? "Mon" is always pronounced Monday, even when I abbreviate it. Even when I see it, I still say the full word. If I write (write "Mr." on chalkboard), what does that mean? Mister. Does it change the name of the man to whom I am referring? No. It's a way of properly addressing an adult male in written letters and when you shake his hand. When you read it or say it, the abbreviation still means "Mister."

What does it mean when you write an X on something? It's something like an abbreviation, but it could have several meanings because it is used to communicate a lot of things. An X is usually used to note when something should not be there. Teachers may use it when they write on your homework to let you know you answered something incorrectly. I've seen it used as an abbreviation on road signs to denote railroad crossings. It looked like this (write "RRX" on the chalkboard). Why do you think it is used on a road sign? It's because writing it out would take up a lot of space, and when you are looking at a sign from a distance, it may be hard to read all those letters on a sign from a far away. But RRX can be written in large letters and be seen clearly from far away.

Have you ever heard of a man who used the name X? Yes, Malcolm X. Do you know what his name was before he changed it to X? It was Little. (Write "Malcolm Little" on the chalkboard.) So when I put the X on Little (draw an X on the name Little), you can see that he used the X to take the place of Little. He did this because he didn't want that name to define him anymore.

What is this word? (Write "Christmas.") There are some people who write it like this. (Draw an X through "Christ" in "Christmas"). Some people say this is how you abbreviate Christmas. Did you notice which word the X is taking the place of? The X replaced Christ. Have you ever listened to people pronounce this abbreviation? They say EXmas. If this was a true abbreviation, like Monday or Mister, you would think that it would be pronounced Christmas.

The truth is, this is not an abbreviation for Christmas. It's a way for people who do not believe in Christ to celebrate Christmas without defining it as Christ's birthday, like Little no longer defined Malcolm's identity.

The word *Xmas* is void of Christ. Christmas is and will always be defined by Christ's birth. So if you are ever told to write the word

Christmas, spell it out completely. If you ever see the word *Xmas,* remember to say "Christmas" so you will always remember the reason we celebrate the season.

Father, may we always remember that Christ is the reason for the season. There is no acronym to write it and no abbreviated way to say it. Christmas is and will always be the day you introduced Christ to the world. In his name we pray. Amen.

GLOSSARY OF IMAGES

Photographs and designs of scripture and other pages for the sermons were done by Adrienne Edwards unless otherwise indicated.

Cover

The author's Bible and kitchen basting syringe

"The Reliable Source"

Author's Bible and the Bible directory

"Upstream Living"

Stream in Rock Creek Park flowing alongside Beach Drive in Washington DC

"A Designer Label"

Computer-generated design of a fabricated designer label

"Living with the Spirit"

Photo of the sky in Washington DC by Justin Smoot

"The Vine and the Branches"

Dead tree branch lying in author's backyard

"Crowns"

A crown made from gift wrap ribbon used as a prop when the sermon was shared with children at Zion Baptist Church in Washington DC

"Crying and Rejoicing"

A computer-generated sunrise of smiley faces, leaving sad faces of the night

"Onions and Lilies"

Photograph of a lily in a bouquet of flowers at Zion Baptist Church by Oceola Briscoe and photograph of an onion by Adrienne Edwards

"Building a Holy Temple"

Photograph of bricks, mortar, and stone

"Giving Thanks before Meals"

Photograph of open Bible as background for the prayer

"Jonah Moments"

Photograph of front walk of the author's home

"Our Church Covenant"

Excerpt from the church covenant adapted by Zion Baptist Church, Washington DC

"Booster Shots"

Bible and needle photographs that were also used for the cover

"The Shoe Shine"

Photograph of a battery-powered candle

"A Kingdom Building Conflict"

Photographs of coffee, bagel, bread, and perfume decanter

"Christ Is Christmas"

Crystal Nativity figurine photographed against a black trash bag

Printed in the United States
By Bookmasters